2   Easy Cabled Scarf
4   Simple Hat
6   Simsbury Shrug
9   Dobbs Ferry Cowl
10 Old Bridge Poncho
12 Jutka Cardigan
17 Striped Cowl
18 Quick Hat
19 Ellis Scarf
20 Easy Cozy Cardi
23 Minerva Super Scarf
24 Lady Violet's Shawl
26 Boro Park Cowl & Headband
28 Exaggerated Raglan Pullover
32 Ridgefield Ruana
35 Pod Stitch Cowl
36 Garfield Ridge Afghan
38 Mitford Hood
40 Classic Ribbed Hat & Scarf
42 Reading Room Cardigan
46 Hudson Cowl
47 3 Strand Grande Shawl
48 High Plains Scarf
49 Quick Seed Stitch Cowl
50 Snowball Hat
52 Betania Cardigan

Easy Cabled Scarf

Easy

MEASUREMENTS
Approx 9½ x 65"/24 x 165cm

MATERIALS
Yarn
LION BRAND® Thick & Quick® Bonus Bundle®, 12oz/340g skeins, each approx 223yd/204m (acrylic) 6
- 2 skeins in #098 Fisherman

Needles
- One pair size 13 (9mm) knitting needles, *or size to obtain gauge*

Notions
- Cable needle
- Pompom maker
- Stitch marker
- Tapestry needle

GAUGE
12 sts + 10 rows = approx 4"/10cm over pattern Rows 1–4 using size 13 (9mm) needles. *BE SURE TO CHECK YOUR GAUGE.*

STITCH GLOSSARY
2/2 LC (2 over 2 left cross) Slip 2 sts to cable needle and hold in front of work, k2, then k2 from cable needle.

NOTES
1) Scarf is worked in one piece, back and forth in rows.
2) When the pattern tells you to slip a st, slip as if to knit or as if to purl, whichever look you prefer.

SCARF
Cast on 30 sts.
Row 1 (RS) Slip 1, *k4, p2; rep from * to last 5 sts, k4, p1.
Row 2 Slip 1, *p4, k2; rep from* to last 5 sts, p5.
Row 3 Slip 1, *2/2 LC, p2; rep from * to last 5 sts, 2/2 LC, p1.
Row 4 Rep Row 2.
Rep Rows 1–4 until piece measures about 65"/165cm from beginning. Bind off.

FINISHING
Following package directions, make 4 pompoms. Tie a pom-pom to each corner of the Scarf.
Weave in ends.•

Simple Hat

●● Easy

MEASUREMENTS
Circumference Approx 18½"/47cm, will stretch to fit a range of sizes
Height Approx 11"/28cm

MATERIALS
Yarn
LION BRAND® Wool-Ease® Thick & Quick®, 6oz/170g skeins, each approx 106yd/97m (acrylic/wool)
- 2 skeins in #612 Coney Island (A)
- 1 skein in #133 Pumpkin (B)

Needles
- One set (5) double-pointed needles (dpn) size 11 (8mm), *or size to obtain gauge*

Notions
- Stitch marker
- Pompom maker
- Tapestry needle

GAUGE
9 sts = approx 4"/10cm over St st worked in the round using size 11 (8mm) needles. *BE SURE TO CHECK YOUR GAUGE.*

NOTES
1) Hat is worked in one piece in the round on double pointed knitting needles. If you prefer, you can work the hat on a 16"/40.5cm long circular needle, then change to double pointed needles to work the last round.
2) The pompom is tied onto finished Hat.

HAT
With A, cast 42 sts onto 4 of the double pointed needles—with 10 sts on each of 2 needles and 11 sts on each of 2 needles.
Place marker for the beginning of the round. Join by working the first stitch on the left hand needle with the working yarn from the right hand needle and being careful not to twist the stitches.
Work in St st worked in the round (knit every stitch on every round) until Hat is approx 11"/28cm long.
Last Round *K2tog; rep from * around—you'll have 21 sts.
Thread yarn tail into tapestry needle and draw through remaining sts. Pull to gather, then knot securely.

FINISHING
With B and following package instructions, make a pompom.
Tie pompom to the top of the Hat.
Weave in yarn ends.●

Simsbury Shrug

●●
Easy

MEASUREMENTS
Width (at widest, before folding and seaming) Approx 59"/150cm
Length Approx 30"/76cm

MATERIALS
Yarn
LION BRAND® Hometown USA®, 5oz/142g skeins, each approx 81yd/74m (acrylic or acrylic/rayon)
- 2 skeins in #219 Northfolk Merlot (A)
- 6 skeins in #312 San Francisco Tweed (B)

Needle
- One size 13 (9mm) circular needle, 29"/73.5cm long, *or size to obtain gauge*

Notion
- Tapestry needle

GAUGE
9½ sts = approx 4"/10cm over St st using size 13 (9mm) needle.
BE SURE TO CHECK YOUR GAUGE.

K1, P1 Rib
(worked over an odd number of sts)
Row 1 (RS) P1, *k1, p1; rep from * to end of row.
Row 2 K the knit sts and p the purl sts.
Rep Row 2 for K1, P1 Rib.

NOTES
1) Shrug is worked in one piece.
2) Piece is folded and seamed following a diagram (see page 8).
3) A circular needle is used to accommodate the large number of sts. Work back and forth in rows as if working with straight needles.

SHRUG
Front and Neck Ribbing
With A, cast on 147 sts.
Work in K1, P1 Rib until piece measures approx 6"/15cm from beginning, end with a WS row as the last row you work.

Body
Change to B.
Dec Row 1 (RS) [K1, p1] twice (for ribbed side edge), [k11, k2tog] 10 times, k to last 4 sts, [p1, k1] twice (for ribbed side edge)—you will have 137 sts at the end of this row.
Row 2 [P1, k1] twice, p to last 4 sts, [k1, p1] twice.
Dec row 3 (RS) [K1, p1] twice, k1, ssk, k to last 7 sts, k2tog, k1, [p1, k1] twice—135 sts.

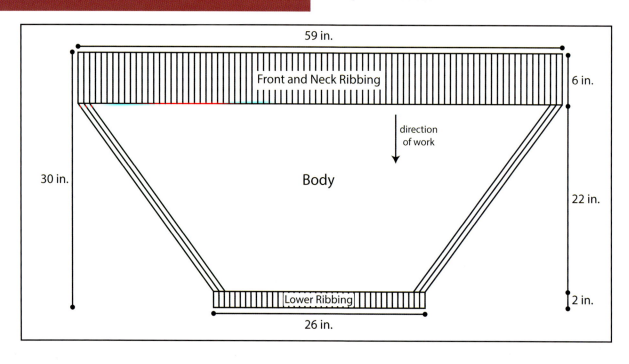

Simsbury Shrug

Rep Rows 2 and 3 until 63 sts remain, end with a Row 3 as the last row you work.

Lower Ribbing
Work in K1, P1 Rib for approx 2"/5cm.
Bind off.

FINISHING
Lay piece onto a flat surface. Following diagram, fold top corners down so that top 2"/5cm of ribbed side edges (A) match side edges of lower ribbing (B). Sew side edges of lower ribbing to ribbed side edges of body. Weave in ends.•

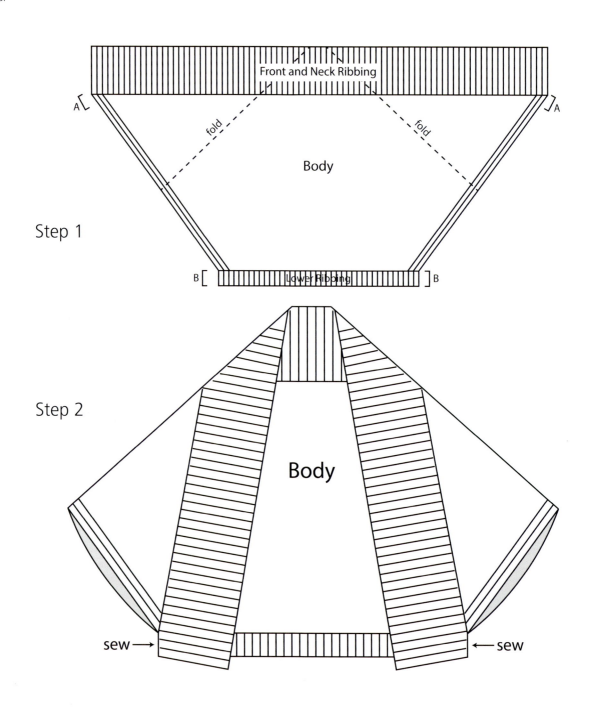

Dobbs Ferry Cowl

●●
Easy

MEASUREMENTS
Circumference Approx 35"/89cm
Height Approx 19"/48.5cm

MATERIALS
Yarn
LION BRAND® Wool-Ease® Thick & Quick®, 6oz/170g skeins, each approx 106yd/97m (acrylic/wool)
- 6 skeins in #098 Linen

Needles
- One size 19 (15mm) circular needle, 29"/73.5cm long, or size to obtain gauge

Notions
- Stitch marker
- Tapestry needle

GAUGE
5 sts = 4"/10cm in St st worked in the rnd (k every rnd) with 3 strands held tog using size 19 (15mm) needle. *BE SURE TO CHECK YOUR GAUGE.*

NOTE
Cowl is worked with 3 strands of yarn held together throughout.

K2, P2 RIB
(multiple of 4 sts)
Rnd 1 *K2, p2; rep from * around.
Rep Rnd 1 for K2, P2 Rib.

COWL
With 3 strands of yarn held tog, cast on 44 sts. Join, being careful not to twist sts. Place marker for beg of rnd.
Work in K2, P2 Rib for 3 rnds.
Change to St st worked in the rnd (k every rnd), and work until piece measures approx 17"/43cm from beg.
Work in K2, P2 Rib for 3 rnds.
Bind off. Weave in ends.•

Old Bridge Poncho

Basic

MEASUREMENTS
Approx 19 x 52"/48.5 x 132cm, before folding and seaming

MATERIALS
Yarn
LION BRAND® Wool-Ease® Thick & Quick® Bonus Bundle®, 12oz/340g skeins, each approx 212yd/194m (acrylic/wool)
• 3 skeins in #618 Bedrock

Needle
• One size 13 (9mm) circular knitting needle, 29"/73.5cm long, *or size to obtain gauge*

Notion
• Tapestry needle

GAUGE
10½ sts + 16 rows = approx 4"/10cm over pat Rows 1–4 using size 13 (9mm) needle. *BE SURE TO CHECK YOUR GAUGE.*

NOTES
1) Poncho is worked in one piece, then seamed.
2) A circular needle is used to accommodate the large number of sts. Work back and forth on the circular needle as if working on straight needles.

PONCHO
Cast on 50 sts.
Row 1 (RS) K2, *p1, k2; rep from * to end of row.
Row 2 P2, *k1, p2; rep from * to end of row.
Row 3 K2, *p4, k2; rep from * to end of row.
Row 4 P2, *k4, p2; rep from * to end of row.
Rep Rows 1–4 until your piece measures approx 52"/132cm from beginning, end with a Row 4 as the last row you work.
Bind off.

FINISHING
Following diagram, sew cast on edge to side edge of Poncho. Weave in ends.•

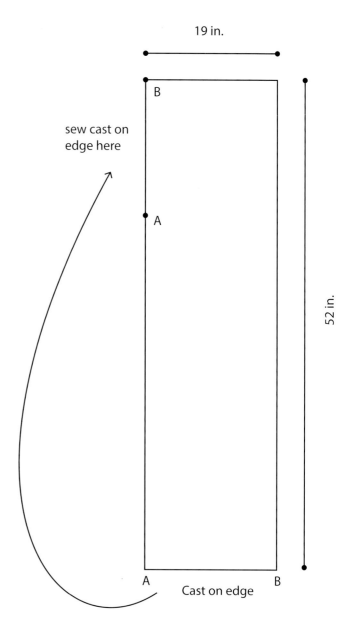

Jutka Cardigan

●●
Easy

SIZES
S (M, L, 1X, 2X).

MEASUREMENTS
Bust (buttoned) Approx 40 (44, 48, 52, 56)"/101.5 (112, 122, 132, 142)cm
Length Approx 21½ (23, 24½, 26, 27½)"/54.5 (58.5, 62, 66, 70)cm

MATERIALS
Yarn
LION BRAND® Wool-Ease® Thick & Quick®, 6oz/170g skeins, each approx 106yd/97m (acrylic/wool)
- 5 (6, 7, 8, 9) skeins in #536 Fossil

Needle
- One size 13 (9mm) circular knitting needle, 40"/101.5cm long, *or size to obtain gauge*

Notions
- Stitch markers
- Tapestry needle

GAUGE
8 sts + 17 rows = approx 4"/10cm in Garter st using size 13 (9mm) needle. *BE SURE TO CHECK YOUR GAUGE.*

STITCH GLOSSARY
M1 (make 1) An increase worked by lifting the horizontal strand lying between needles and placing it onto the left needle. Knit this new stitch through the back loop—1 st increased.

CABLE CAST-ON
*Insert right needle between first 2 sts on left needle, wrap yarn and pull through (as if knitting a st), transfer new st to left needle; rep from * for desired number of sts.

NOTES
1) Cardigan is worked in 3 pieces: Body and 2 Sleeves.
2) The Back is knit first from back neck down to underarms, then front edge of armholes. Increases are worked at the beginning and end of rows to shape front shoulders and on each side of markers placed at underarms to shape lower body. When front shoulders are complete, decreases are worked at the beginning and end of rows to shape front neck.
3) A circular needle is used to accommodate the number of sts. Work back and forth in rows with the circular needle as if working on straight needles.
4) When you see "work even" in the instructions, this means to continue on in the pattern st you have established without changing the st count by increasing, decreasing, casting on, or binding off.

CARDIGAN
Back
Beg at back neck, cast on 14 (14, 16, 16, 18) sts.
Knit 1 row.

Shape back shoulders
Row 1 Cable cast-on 5 (5, 6, 6, 7) sts, k to end of row—you will have 19 (19, 22, 22, 25) sts in this row.
Row 2 Cable cast-on 5 (5, 6, 6, 7) sts, k to end of row—24 (24, 28, 28, 32) sts.
Rows 3–6 Cable cast-on 4 (5, 5, 6, 6) sts, k to end of row—40 (44, 48, 52, 56) sts in Row 6.
Work even in Garter st (k every st on every row) until piece measures approx 10½ (11, 11½, 12, 12½)"/26.5 (28, 29, 30.5, 32)cm from beg.

Cast on for front armholes
Rows 1 and 2 Cable cast-on 18 (19, 20, 21, 22) sts, k to end of row—76 (82, 88, 94, 100) sts in Row 2.

Shape fronts, front shoulders, and lower body
Row 1 (RS) K16 (17, 18, 19, 20), yo, k1, pm, k1, yo, k40 (44, 48, 52, 56), yo, k1, pm, k1, yo, k16 (17, 18, 19, 20)—80 (86, 92, 98, 104) sts.
Row 2 Knit, slipping markers as you come to them (continue to slip markers, as you come to them, to end of piece).
Note Increases (M1) at beg and end of rows shapes front shoulders, yarn overs (yo) shape fronts and lower body.
Inc Row 3 K1, M1, k to 1 st before first marker, yo, k1, sm, k1, yo, k to 1 st before next marker, yo, k1, sm, k1, yo, k to last st, M1, k1—86 (92, 98, 104, 110) sts.
Row 4 Knit.
Row 5 K to 1 st before first marker, yo, k1, sm, k1, yo, k to 1 st before next marker, yo, k1, sm, k1, yo, k to end of row—90 (96, 102, 108, 114) sts.
Rows 6–7 (6–9, 6–11, 6–13, 6–15) Rep Rows 4 and 5 for 1 (2, 3, 4, 5) more times—94 (104, 114, 124, 134) sts.

Jutka Cardigan

Rep last 2 rows until piece measures approx 6½ (7½, 8, 9, 9½)"/16.5 (19, 20.5, 23, 24)cm from front armhole cast-on, end with a WS row as the last row you work.

Shape front neck and lower body
Row 1 (RS) Bind off 5 (5, 6, 6, 7) sts, k to 1 st before first marker, yo, k1, sm, k1, yo, k to 1 st before next marker, yo, k1, sm, k1, yo, k to end of row.
Row 2 Bind off 5 (5, 6, 6, 7) sts, k to end of row.
Row 3 K1, ssk, k to 1 st before first marker, yo, k1, sm, k1, yo, k to 1 st before next marker, yo, k1, sm, k1, yo, k to last 3 sts, k2tog, k1—2 sts increased.
Row 4 Knit.
Rows 5–8 Rep Rows 3 and 4 for 2 more times.
Row 9 K to 1 st before first marker, yo, k1, sm, k1, yo, k to 1 st before next marker, yo, k1, sm, k1, yo, k to end of row.
Row 10 Knit.
Rows 11–20 (11–20, 11–22, 11–22, 11–24) Rep Rows 9 and 10 for 5 (5, 6, 6, 7) more times.
Bind off as if to knit.

Sleeves (make 2)
Cast on 32 (34, 36, 38, 40) sts.
Knit 6 rows.
Inc Row K1, M1, k to last st, M1, k1—34 (36, 38, 40, 42) sts.
Knit 7 rows.
Inc Row K1, M1, k to last st, M1, k1—36 (38, 40, 42, 44) sts.
Knit 5 rows.

Shape Cap
Rows 1–8 Bind off 3 (3, 3, 4, 4) sts, k to end of row—12 (14, 16, 10, 12) sts.
Bind off rem sts as if to knit.

FINISHING
Sew shoulder seams.

Neck Trim
From RS, pick up and k 48 (48, 54, 54, 69) sts evenly spaced along neck edge. Bind off, without working any rows.

Sew in Sleeves. Sew Sleeve seams.
Weave in ends.•

Next Row Knit.
Next Row (RS) Rep Row 3—100 (110, 120, 130, 140) sts.
Next 6 (8, 10, 12, 14) Rows Beg at Row 4, rep last 6 (8, 10, 12, 14) rows—114 (128, 142, 156, 170) sts when all increases have been completed.
Next Row Knit.
Next Row K to 1 st before first marker, yo, k1, sm, k1, yo, k to 1 st before next marker, yo, k1, sm, k1, yo, k to end of row—118 (132, 146, 160, 174) sts.

Step 1: Back

Step 2: Cast On for Front Armholes

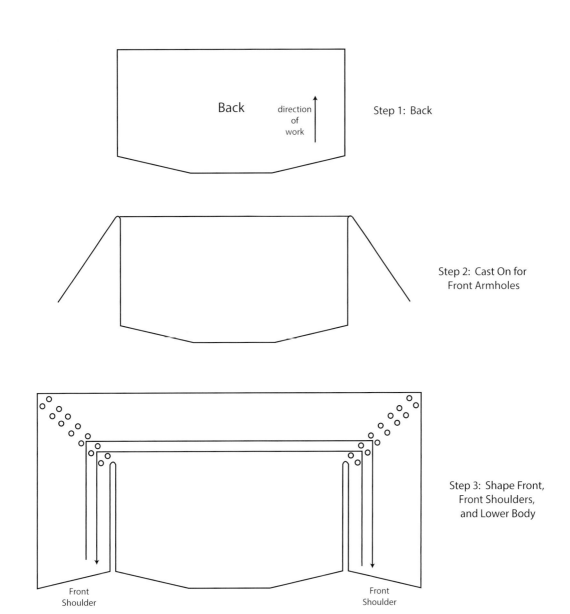

Step 3: Shape Front, Front Shoulders, and Lower Body

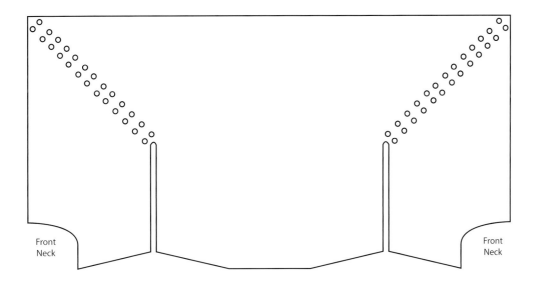

Step 4: Shape Front Neck, and Continue Shaping Lower Body

Jutka Cardigan

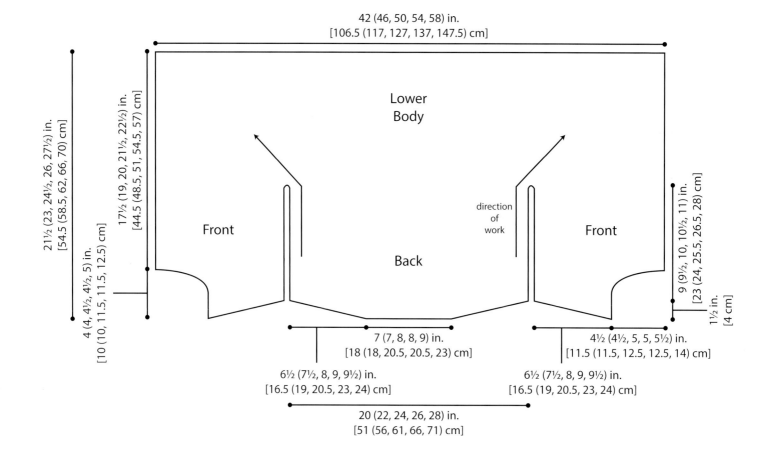

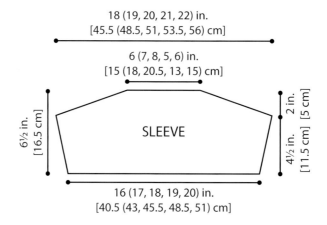

Striped Cowl

Easy

MEASUREMENTS
Circumference Approx 76"/193cm
Width Approx 11"/28cm

MATERIALS
Yarn
LION BRAND® Wool-Ease® Thick & Quick®, 6oz/170g skeins, each approx 106yd/97m (acrylic/wool)
- 1 skein in #506 Blackstone (A)
- 1 skein in #138 Cranberry (B)
- 1 skein in #154 Grey Marble (C)

Needles
- One pair size 15 (10mm) knitting needles, *or size to obtain gauge*

Notion
- Tapestry needle

GAUGE
8 sts = approx 4"/10cm in St st using size 15 (10mm) needles.
BE SURE TO CHECK YOUR GAUGE.

NOTES
1) Cowl is worked in one piece, back and forth in rows as a rectangle, then ends are sewn together to make a ring.
2) The yarn color is changed to make stripes. Carry unused color along side edge of piece until next needed.
3) Side edges of the Cowl will roll gently—this is part of the design of the Cowl!

COWL
With A, cast on 22 sts.
Work in St st (k on RS, p on WS), working 2 rows with A then 2 rows with B, until you have worked 18 B stripes.
Cut A, join C.
Continue in St st, working 2 rows with C then 2 rows with B, until you have worked 18 C stripes.
Cut B, join A.
Continue in St st, working 2 rows with A then 2 rows with C, until you have worked 18 C stripes.
Work 2 rows with A, then bind off.

FINISHING
Sew cast-on end to bound-off end to make a ring.
Weave in ends.•

Quick Hat

Easy

MEASUREMENTS
Circumference Approx 19"/48.5cm, will stretch to fit a range of sizes
Height Approx 10"/25.5cm

MATERIALS
LION BRAND® Mandala® Thick & Quick®, 5 1/3oz/150g cakes, each approx 87yd/79m (acrylic)
• 1 cake in #200 Labyrinth

Needles
• One size 13 (9mm) circular knitting needle, 16"/40.5cm long, *or size to obtain gauge*
• One set (5) size 13 (9mm) double-pointed needles (dpn)

Notions
• Stitch marker
• Tapestry needle

GAUGE
8 sts = approx 4"/10cm over St st worked in the round using size 13 (9mm) needles. *BE SURE TO CHECK YOUR GAUGE.*

NOTE
Hat is made in one piece in the round, beginning on a circular knitting needle, then changing to double pointed knitting needles when sts are decreased.

HAT
With circular needle, cast on 40 sts.
Place marker for the beginning of the round and join by working the first stitch on the left hand needle with the working yarn from the right hand needle and being careful not to twist the stitches.
Rnd 1 *K1, p1; rep from * around.
Rnds 2–5 Rep Rnd 1.
Change to St st worked in the round (knit all sts on every round), and work until piece measures approx 9"/23cm from beginning.

Shape Crown
Note As you work the next round, change to double pointed needles. Don't forget to move the beginning of round marker onto the double pointed needles!
Next Rnd *K2tog; rep from * around—you'll have 20 sts.
Next Rnd Knit.
Last Rnd *K2tog; rep from * around—you'll have 10 sts.
Cut yarn, leaving a long yarn tail.
Thread yarn tail into tapestry needle and draw through remaining sts. Pull to close top of Hat, then knot securely.

FINISHING
Weave in ends.•

Ellis Scarf

●●
Easy

MEASUREMENTS
Approx 8 x 72"/20.5 x 183cm

MATERIALS
Yarn
LION BRAND® Wool-Ease® Thick & Quick® Bonus Bundle®, 12oz/340g skeins, each approx 212yd/194m (acrylic/wool)
- 2 skeins in #539 Toasted Almond

Needles
- One pair size 13 (9mm) knitting needles, *or size to obtain gauge*

Notion
- Tapestry Needle

GAUGE
8 sts = approx 4"/10cm over pat rows 1 and 2 using size 13 (9mm) needles. *BE SURE TO CHECK YOUR GAUGE.*

NOTES
1) Scarf is worked in once piece.
2) Slip all slip sts as if to purl wyif.
3) With yarn in front (wyif) refers to the side of the work facing you as you work the row. To move the yarn from front to back or back to front, bring yarn between your needles, being careful not to wrap yarn over the needle.

SCARF
Cast on 19 sts.
Row 1 (RS) Slip 1, k17, p1.
Row 2 *Wyif, slip 1 as if to purl, k2; rep from * to last st, purl the last st.
Rep rows 1 and 2 until piece measures approx 72"/183cm from beginning, end with a Row 1 as the last row you work. Bind off.

FINISHING
Weave in ends.●

Easy Cozy Cardi

Easy

SIZES
S/L (1X/2X).

MEASUREMENTS
Bust Approx 47 (55)"/119.5 (139.5)cm
Back Length Approx 27 (28)"/68.5 (71)cm
Front Length Approx 23 (24)"/58.5 (61)cm

MATERIALS
Yarn
LION BRAND® Wool-Ease® Thick & Quick®, 6oz/170g skeins, each approx 106yd/97m (acrylic/wool)
• 10 (12) skeins in #536 Fossil

Needles
• One pair size 13 (9mm) knitting needles, *or size to obtain gauges*

Notion
• Tapestry needle

GAUGES
10 sts + 12 rows = approx 4"/10cm in St st using size 13 (9mm) needles.
9 sts + 12 rows = approx 4"/10cm in Seed st using size 13 (9mm) needles. BE SURE TO CHECK YOUR GAUGES.

SEED STITCH
(worked over an even number of sts)
Row 1 *K1, p1; rep from * to end of row.
Row 2 P the knit sts, and k the purl sts.
Rep Row 2 for Seed st.

(worked over an odd number of sts)
Row 1 *K1, p1; rep from * to last st, k1.
Row 2 P the knit sts, and k the purl sts.
Rep Row 2 for Seed st.

NOTES
1) Cardi is made in 5 pieces: Back, Left and Right Fronts, and 2 Sleeves.
2) The collar is worked from stitches picked up around neck edge.
3) The back of the Cardi is longer than the fronts.

CARDI
Back
Cast on 53 (62) sts.
Work in Seed st until piece measures approx 16"/40.5cm from beg. Beg with a RS (knit) row, work in St st (k on RS, p on WS) until piece measures approx 25 (26)"/63.5 (66)cm from beg, end with a WS (purl) row as the last row you work.

Shape shoulders
Row 1 (RS) Bind off 5 (6) sts, k to end of row—you will have 48 (56) sts in this row.
Row 2 Bind off 5 (6) sts, p to end of row—43 (50) sts.
Rows 3–6 Rep Rows 1 and 2 twice—23 (26) sts when all bind-offs are complete.
Bind off.

Left Front
Cast on 29 (33) sts.
Work in Seed st until piece measures approx 12"/30.5cm from beg, end with a WS row as the last row you work.
Next Row (RS) K to last 3 sts, work in Seed st over last 3 sts for front border.
Next Row Work in Seed st over first 3 sts, p to end of row.
Rep last 2 rows until piece measures approx 21 (22)"/53.5 (56)cm from beg, end with a RS row as the last row you work.

Shape neck and shoulders
Row 1 (WS) Bind off 7 sts for neck, p to end of row—22 (26) sts.
Row 2 Bind off 5 (6) sts for shoulder, k to end of row—17 (20) sts.
Row 3 Bind off 4 (5) sts for neck, p to end of row—13 (15) sts.
Row 4 Bind off 5 (6) sts for shoulder, k to end of row—8 (9) sts.
Row 5 Bind off 3 sts for neck, p to end of row—5 (6) sts.
Bind off rem sts for shoulder.

Right Front
Cast on 29 (33) sts.
Work in Seed st until piece measures about 12"/30.5cm from beg, end with a WS row as the last row you work.
Next Row (RS) Work in Seed st over first 3 sts for front border, k to end of row.
Next Row P to last 3 sts, work in Seed st over last 3 sts.
Rep last 2 rows until piece measures same as Left Front to Neck and Shoulder shaping, end with a WS row as the last row you work.

Easy Cozy Cardi

Shape neck and shoulders
Row 1 (RS) Bind off 7 sts for neck, k to end of row—22 (26) sts.
Row 2 Bind off 5 (6) sts for shoulder, p to end of row—17 (20) sts.
Row 3 Bind off 4 (5) sts for neck, k to end of row—13 (15) sts.
Row 4 Bind off 5 (6) sts for shoulder, p to end of row—8 (9) sts.
Row 5 Bind off 3 sts for neck, k to end of row—5 (6) sts.
Bind off rem sts for shoulder.

Sleeves (make 2)
Cast on 35 (39) sts.
Work in Seed st until piece measures approx 12"/30.5cm from beg.

Shape sleeve cap
Next Row (RS) Knit.
Continue in St st for 3 more rows.
Next Row (RS) Bind off 2 sts, k to end of row—33 (37) sts.
Continue in St st and bind off 2 sts at the beg of EVERY row until 3 sts rem.
Bind off.

FINISHING
Sew Fronts to Back at shoulders.

Collar
From RS, pick up and k 56 (64) sts evenly spaced around neck edge.
Row 1 (WS) K1, *p2, k2; rep from * to last 3 sts, p2, k1.
Row 2 K the knit sts and p the purl sts.
Rep Row 2 until collar measures approx 4"/10cm.
Bind off in pattern.

Sew in Sleeves. Sew side (Back is approx 4"/10cm longer than Front at sides) and Sleeve seams.
Weave in ends.•

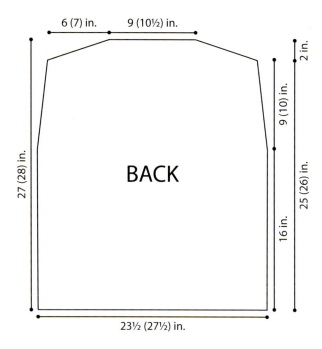

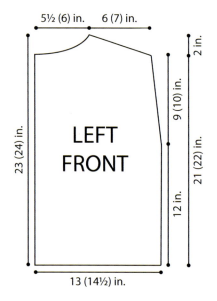

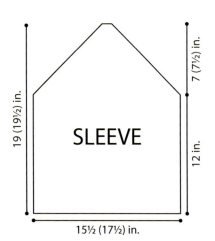

Minerva Super Scarf

Basic

MEASUREMENTS
Approx 11 x 98"/28 x 249cm

MATERIALS
Yarn
LION BRAND® Homespun® Thick & Quick®, 8oz/227g skeins, each approx 160yd/146m (acrylic/polyester)
- 2 skeins in #211 Granite Stripes (A)
- 1 skein in #312 Edwardian (B)

Needles
- One pair size 15 (10mm) knitting needles, *or size to obtain gauge*

Notion
- Tapestry needle

GAUGE
9 sts = approx 4"/10cm over garter st using size 15 (10mm) needles. *BE SURE TO CHECK YOUR GAUGE.*

NOTE
Scarf is worked in one piece with 2 colors of yarn.

SCARF
With A, cast on 24 sts.
Work in Garter st (knit every st on every row) until piece measures approx 61"/155cm from beginning.

The rest of the Scarf is worked by changing yarn color —working 2 rows in each color.
You don't need to cut the yarn between color changes, just carry the color yarn that you are not using along the side edge of the Scarf. Continue in Garter st, working 2 rows with B and 2 rows with A alternately until Scarf measures approx 98"/249cm from beginning. Bind off.

FINISHING
Weave in ends.•

Lady Violet's Shawl

●●
Easy

MEASUREMENTS
Approx 22 x 50"/56 x 127cm at widest and longest points

MATERIALS
Yarn
LION BRAND® Wool-Ease® Thick & Quick®, 6oz/170g skeins, each approx 106yd/97m (acrylic/wool)
• 3 skeins in #308 Starlight

Needle
• One size 15 (10mm) circular needle, 29"/73.5cm long, *or size to obtain gauge*

Notions
• Stitch markers
• Tapestry needle

GAUGE
8 sts + 11½ rows = approx 4"/10cm over Rows 1–12 using size 15 (10mm) needle. *BE SURE TO CHECK YOUR GAUGE.*

NOTES
1) Shawl begins at center back neck and is shaped by working yarn over (yo) increases.
2) A yarn over creates a new loop on your needle and is worked by wrapping the yarn around your right hand needle. Do not use an existing st to make a yarn over. The finished yarn over will leave an open space (like an eyelet) in your knitting—that is part of this design.
3) The first and last 2 sts of every row are always knit.
4) A circular needle is used to accommodate the large number of sts. Work back and forth on circular needle as if working on straight needles.

SHAWL
Cast on 5 sts.
Rows 1 and 2 Knit.
Row 3 K1, kfb, k1, kfb, k1—you will have 7 sts at the end of Row 3.
Row 4 Knit.
Row 5 (RS) K2, yo, k1, yo, pm, k1, pm, yo, k1, yo, k2—11 sts.
Row 6 K2, yo, k to last 2 sts slipping markers as you come to them, yo, k2—13 sts.
Row 7 K2, yo, k to marker, yo, sm, k1, sm, yo, k to last 2 sts, yo, k2—17 sts.
Rows 8–31 Rep Rows 6 and 7 twelve times—89 sts at the end of Row 31.
Row 32 (WS) Knit.
Row 33 Rep Row 7—93 sts.
Rows 34 and 35 Rep Rows 32 and 33—97 sts at the end of Row 35.
Row 36 Knit.
Eyelet Row 37 (RS) K2, yo, k1, *yo, k2tog; rep from * to 1 st before marker, k1, yo, sm, k1, sm, yo, k1, **k2tog, yo; rep from ** to last 3 sts, k1, yo, k2—101 sts.
Rows 38–43 Rep Rows 32 and 33 three times—113 sts at the end of Row 43.
Rows 44–59 Rep Rows 36–43 twice—145 sts at the end of Row 59.
Rows 60 and 61 Rep Rows 36 and 37—149 sts at the end of Row 61.
Row 62 Knit.
Row 63 Rep Row 7—153 sts.
Bind off.

FINISHING
Weave in ends.●

Boro Park Cowl & Headband

Easy

MEASUREMENTS
Cowl
Circumference Approx 26"/66cm
Height Approx 13"/33cm
Headband
Circumference Approx 17"/43cm, will stretch to fit a range of sizes
Height Approx 4½"/11.5cm

MATERIALS
Yarn
LION BRAND® Wool-Ease® Thick & Quick® Bonus Bundle®, 12oz/340g skeins, each approx 212yd/194m (acrylic/wool)
• 1 skein in #616 Urban Camo

Needles
• One pair size 17 (13mm) knitting needles, *or size to obtain gauge*

Notion
• Tapestry needle

GAUGE
8 sts = approx 4"/10cm in Garter st using size 17 (13mm) needles.
BE SURE TO CHECK YOUR GAUGE.

NOTES
1) Cowl is worked in 2 sections and then sewn together.
2) Stitches for the second section are picked up from the first section.
3) Headband is worked in one piece and sewn together to make a ring.

COWL
Cast on 26 sts.

First Section
Work in Garter st (knit every st on every row) until piece measures approx 13"/33cm from beginning.
Bind off.

Second Section
Pick up and knit 26 sts evenly spaced along either side edge of the first section.
Work in Garter st until second section measures approx 13"/33cm.
Bind off.

Sew short ends of piece together to make a ring.
Weave in ends.

HEADBAND
Cast on 34 sts.
Work in Garter st until piece measures approx 4½"/11.5cm from beginning.
Bind off leaving a long yarn tail.

Sew ends of piece together to make a ring.
Wrap a length of yarn several times around the Headband and knot.
Weave in ends.•

Exaggerated Raglan Pullover

•• Easy

SIZES
S/M (L/1X).

MEASUREMENTS
Bust Approx 60 (70)"/152.5 (178)cm
Length (at center front, not including collar) Approx 26½ (29½)"/67.5(75)cm

MATERIALS
Yarn
LION BRAND® Wool-Ease® Thick & Quick®, 6oz/170g skeins, each approx 106yd/97m (acrylic/wool)
• 8 (11) skeins in #135 Spice

Needles
• One size 13 (9mm) circular knitting needle, 16"/40.5cm long, *or size to obtain gauge*
• One size 13 (9mm) circular knitting needle, 24"/61cm long
• One size 13 (9mm) circular knitting needle, 40"/101.5cm long
• One set (5) size 13 (9mm) double-pointed needles (dpn)

Notions
• Stitch markers
• Stitch holders
• Tapestry needle

GAUGE
9½ sts + 13 rnds = approx 4"/10cm in St st worked in the round using size 13 (9mm) needles. *BE SURE TO CHECK YOUR GAUGE.*

STITCH GLOSSARY
M1 (make 1) An increase worked by lifting the horizontal strand lying between needles and placing it onto the left needle. Knit this new stitch through the back loop—1 st increased.
M1P (make 1 st as if to purl) An increase worked by lifting the horizontal strand lying between the needles and placing it onto the left needle. Purl this new stitch through the back loop—1 st increased.

K1, P1 RIB
(worked in rnds over an even number of sts)
Rnd 1 *K1, p1; rep from * to end of rnd.
Rnd 2 K the knit sts and p the purl sts.
Rep Rnd 2 for K1, P1 Rib.

NOTES
1) Pullover is worked in the round from the top down.
2) At underarms, work is divided and body and sleeves worked separately.
3) Markers are placed to indicate increase locations for raglans and at center front and back. Use one color markers for raglans and different color markers for center front and back.
4) The ribbed neck is worked from sts picked up around the neck edge of the Pullover.

PULLOVER
With middle length circular needle, cast on 68 sts.
Place marker for beg of rnd. Join by working the first st on left hand needle with the working yarn from the right hand needle and being careful not to twist sts.
Note When placing markers on next rnd, use different color markers for raglans and for center front and back.
Set-up Rnd 1 (RS) K8, pm for raglan, k1, p2, k1, pm for raglan; k7, pm for center front, k1, p2, k1, pm for center front; k7, pm for raglan, k1, p2, k1, pm for raglan, k8, pm for raglan, k1, p2, k1, pm for raglan; k7, pm for center back, k1, p2, k1, pm for center back; k7, pm for raglan, k1, p2, k1, use beg of rnd marker as final raglan marker.
Rnds 2 and 3 *K to marker, sm, k1, p2, k1, sm; rep from * around.
Inc Rnd 4 (Raglan Inc Rnd) M1, k to first (raglan) marker, M1, sm, k1, p2, k1, sm, M1, k to next (front) marker, sm, k1, p2, k1, sm, [k to next (raglan) marker, M1, sm, k1, p2, k1, sm, M1] twice, k to next (back) marker, sm, k1, p2, k1, sm, k to next (raglan) marker, M1, sm, k1, p2, k1, sm—76 sts.
Rnd 5 *K to marker, sm, k1, p2, k1, sm; rep from * around.
Inc Rnd 6 (Raglan and Center Front/Back Inc Rnd) *M1, k to marker, M1, sm, k1, p2, k1, sm; rep from * around—88 sts.
Rnd 7 *K to marker, sm, k1, p2, k1, sm; rep from * around.
Note As you work the following rounds, change to the longer circular needle when you have sufficiently increased the sts.
Rnds 8–15 Rep Rnds 4–7 for 2 more times—128 sts.
Rnd 16 Rep Rnd 4—136 sts.
Rnds 17 and 18 Rep Rnd 5 twice.
Rnd 19 Rep Rnd 4—144 sts.
Rnd 20 Rep Rnd 5.

Exaggerated Raglan Pullover

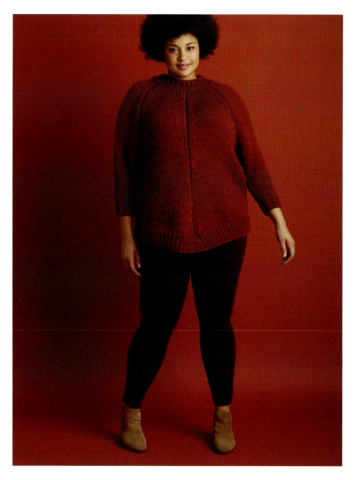

Inc Rnd 21 (Center Front/Back Inc Rnd) K to first marker, sm, k1, p2, k1, sm, k to next (front) marker, M1, sm, k1, p2, k1, sm, M1, [k to next marker, sm, k1, p2, k1, sm] twice, k to next marker (back), M1, sm, k1, p2, k1, sm, M1, k to next marker, sm, k1, p2, k1—148 sts.
Rnd 22 Rep Rnd 4—156 sts.
Rnds 23–25 Rep Rnds 17–19—164 sts in Rnd 25.
Rnds 26 and 27 Rep Rnd 5 twice.
Rnd 28 Rep Rnd 6—176 sts.
Rnds 29–31 Rep Rnds 17–19—184 sts in Rnd 31.
Rnds 32–34 Rep Rnds 17–19—192 sts in Rnd 34.
Rnd 35 Rep Rnd 21—196 sts.
Rnd 36 Rep Rnd 5.
Rnd 37 Rep Rnd 4—204 sts.
Rnds 38–40 Rep Rnds 17–19—212 sts in Rnd 40.
Rnd 41 Rep Rnd 5.
Rnd 42 Rep Rnd 21—216 sts.
Rnds 43–47 (58) Rep Rnds 16–20 (31)—232 (272) sts in last rnd worked.

Divide for Body and Sleeves
Next Rnd *K to marker, sm, k1, p2, k1, sm; rep from * for 4 more times, k to next marker, sm, k1, p2 (you should be 1 st from beg of rnd marker), place next 44 (52) sts on holder for first sleeve, pm for side seam and new beg of rnd marker.

Next Rnd P2, k1, remove marker, k to next marker, sm, k1, p2, k1, sm, k to next marker, remove marker, k1, p2, pm for side seam, place next 44 (52) sts on holder for second sleeve, p2, k1, remove marker, k to next marker, sm, k1, p2, k1, sm, k to next marker, remove marker, k1, p2, sm—you should have 44 (52) sts on each of 2 holders for sleeves and 144 (168) sts rem on needle for body.

Body
Rnd 1 P2, k to next (front) marker, sm, k1, p2, k1, sm, k to 2 sts before next (side) marker, p2, sm, p2, k to next marker, sm, k1, p2, k1, sm, k to last 2 sts, p2, sm.
Inc Rnd 2 (Center Front/Back Inc Rnd) P2, k to next marker, M1, sm, k1, p2, k1, sm, M1, k to 2 sts before next marker, p2, sm, p2, k to next marker, M1, sm, k1, p2, k1, sm, M1, k to last 2 sts, p2, sm—148 (172) sts.
Rnds 3–5 P2, k to next marker, sm, k1, p2, k1, sm, k to 2 sts before next marker, p2, sm, p2, k to next marker, sm, k1, p2, k1, sm, k to last 2 sts, p2, sm.
Rnd 6 (Center Front/Back Inc and Side Seam Dec Rnd) K2tog, k to next marker, M1, sm, k1, p2, k1, sm, M1, k to 2 sts before next marker, k2tog through back loops, sm, k2tog, k to next marker, M1, sm, k1, p2, k1, sm, M1, k to last 2 sts, k2tog through back loops, sm—148 (172) sts.
Rnds 7–9 K to next marker, sm, k1, p2, k1, sm, k to next marker, sm, k to next marker, sm, k1, p2, k1, sm, k to end of rnd, sm.
Inc Rnd 10 (Center Front/Back Inc Rnd) K to next marker, M1, sm, k1, p2, k1, sm, M1, k to next marker, sm, k to next marker, M1, sm, k1, p2, k1, sm, M1, k to end of rnd, sm—152 (176) sts.
Rnd 11 Rep Rnd 7.
Dec Rnd 12 (Side Seam Dec Rnd) K2tog, k to next marker, sm, k1, p2, k1, sm, k to 2 sts before next marker, k2tog through back loops, sm, k2tog, k to next marker, sm, k1, p2, k1, sm, k to last 2 sts, k2tog through back loops, sm—148 (172) sts.
Rnd 13 Rep Rnd 7.
Rnd 14 Rep Rnd 10—152 (176) sts.
Rnds 15–17 Rep Rnd 7.
Rnds 18–29 Rep Rnds 6–17—156 (180) sts when all increases and decreases are completed.
Rnds 30–33 Rep Rnds 6–9.
Rnd 34 Rep Rnd 7.

Lower Ribbing
Remove side seam marker as you work Rnd 1.
Rnd 1 (Set-Up Rnd) *K2tog, p1, [k1, p1] to next marker, remove marker, k1, M1P, pm, k2tog, pm, M1P, k1, remove marker, p1, [k1, p1] to next marker; rep from * once more—156 (180) sts.
Rnd 2 Work in K1, P1 Rib, slipping markers as you come to them.
Rnd 3 (Center Front/Back Increase Rnd) *Work in K1, P1 Rib to next marker, M1, sm, k1, sm, M1; rep from * once more, work in K1, P1 Rib to end of rnd—160 (184) sts.
Rnd 4 *Work in K1, P1 Rib to 1 st before next marker, p1, sm, k1, sm, p1; rep from * once more.

Inc Rnd 5 (Center Front/Back Inc Rnd) *Work in K1, P1 Rib to 1 st before next marker, k1, M1P, sm, k1, sm, M1P, k1; rep from * once more, work in K1, P1 Rib to end of rnd—164 (188) sts.
Next Rnd Work in K1, P1 Rib around, removing front and back markers as you come to them.
Last 2 Rnds Work in K1, P1 Rib.
Bind off in rib.

Sleeves
Place 44 (52) sts of one sleeve onto shorter circular needle. Place marker for beg of rnd. Join by working the first st on the left hand needle with the working yarn from the right hand needle.
Rnds 1 and 2 Knit.
Dec Rnd 3 (Dec Rnd) K1, k2tog through back loops, k to 2 sts before end of rnd, k2tog—42 (50) sts.
Rep Rnds 1–3 for 5 (6) more times—32 (38) sts, changing to double pointed needles when sts have been sufficiently decreased.

Cuff ribbing
Set-Up Rnd 1 *K1, p2tog; rep from * to last 2 sts, k1, p1—22 (26) sts.
Work in K1, P1 Rib for 6 rnds.
Bind off in rib.
Rep for second sleeve.

FINISHING
Ribbed Neck
From RS with shorter circular needle, pick up and k 56 sts evenly spaced around neck edge.
Join by working the first st on the left hand needle with the working yarn from the right hand needle.
Work in K1, P1 Rib for approx 2¾"/7cm.
Bind off in rib.

Sew underarms closed.
Weave in ends.•

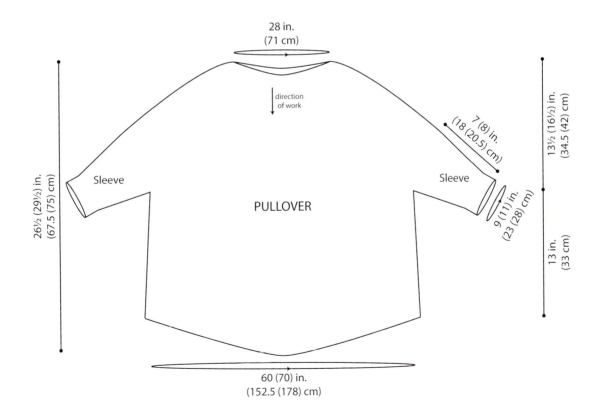

Ridgefield Ruana

Easy

MEASUREMENTS
Width Approx 45"/114.5cm
Length Approx 28"/71cm

MATERIALS
Yarn
LION BRAND® Thick & Quick® Bonus Bundle®, 12oz/340g skeins, each approx 223yd/204m (acrylic)
• 4 skeins in #150 Oxford Grey

Needle
• One size 15 (10mm) circular knitting needle, 29"/73.5cm long, *or size to obtain gauge*

Notions
• Stitch markers
• Cable needle
• Tapestry needle

GAUGE
6 sts + 10 rows = approx 4"/10cm over Garter Rib using size 15 (10mm) needle. *BE SURE TO CHECK YOUR GAUGE.*

STITCH GLOSSARY
4/4 LC (4 over 4 left cross) Slip 4 sts to cable needle and hold in front of work, k4, then k4 from cable needle.

GARTER RIB
(worked over a multiple of 6 sts)
Row 1 (WS) *K3, p3; rep from * across.
Row 2 Knit.
Rep Rows 1 and 2 for Garter Rib.

CABLE PANEL
(worked over 14 sts)
Row 1 (WS) K3, p8, k3.
Row 2 P3, k8, p3.
Rows 3–6 Rep Rows 1 and 2.
Row 7 Rep Row 1.
Row 8 P3, 4/4 LC, p3.
Rows 9–16 Rep Rows 1 and 2.
Rep Rows 1–16 for Cable Panel.

NOTES
1) Two Panels are worked separately, then sewn together to make the Ruana.
2) A circular needle is used to accommodate the large number of stitches. Work back and forth in rows on the circular needle as if working on straight needles.
3) The first stitch of every row is slipped to make an even side edge. Slip as if to knit or purl, whichever you prefer.

RUANA
First Panel
Cast on 34 sts.
Row 1 (WS) Slip 1, pm, work Row 1 of Garter Rib over next 18 sts, pm, work Row 1 of Cable Panel over next 16 sts, pm, p1.
Row 2 Slip 1, sm, work Row 2 of Cable Panel to next marker, sm, work Row 2 of Garter Rib to next marker, sm, p1.
Continue as established, working sts between markers in patterns, and slipping the first st and purling the last st of every row, until piece measures approx 56"/142cm from beginning.
Bind off.

Second Panel
Cast on 34 sts and work same as Panel 1.

FINISHING
Place the 2 Panels side by side with RS facing and Cable Panels at center. Beginning at lower edge, sew Panels together for 28"/71cm. Weave in ends.

Blocking
Dampen Ruana thoroughly. Spread a towel onto a flat surface, then lay Ruana onto towel and smooth into shape. Gently shape to match finished measurements. Allow to air dry.•

Ridgefield Ruana

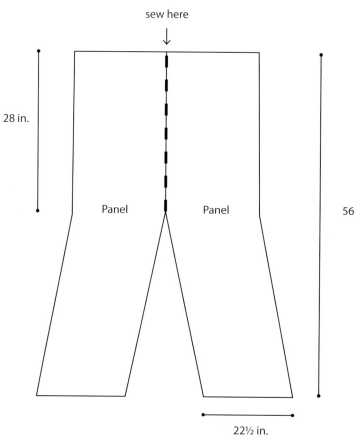

sew here

28 in.

Panel Panel

56

22½ in.

Pod Stitch Cowl

Easy

MEASUREMENTS
Circumference Approx 28"/71cm
Height Approx 10½"/27cm

MATERIALS
Yarn
LION BRAND® Wool-Ease® Thick & Quick® Bonus Bundle®, 12oz/340g skeins, each approx 212yd/194m (acrylic/wool) (6)
- 1 skein in #154 Grey Marble

Needle
- One size 13 (9mm) circular needle, 29"/73.5cm long, *or size to obtain gauge*

Notions
- Stitch marker
- Tapestry needle

GAUGE
12 sts = approx 4"/10cm in Pod Stitch using size 13 (9mm) needle.
EXACT GAUGE IS NOT ESSENTIAL FOR THIS PROJECT.

STITCH GLOSSARY
k5tog Knit 5 sts together—4 sts decreased.
M1P (make 1 st as if to purl) Lift the horizontal thread lying between the needles and placing it onto the left needle. Purl this new stitch through the back loop—1 st increased.
(p1, k1, p1) in next st Purl in next st but do not remove st from needle. Take yarn to back between needles, knit the same st, but do not remove st from needle. Bring yarn to front between needles, purl the same st and remove st from needle—2 sts increased.

POD STITCH
(multiple of 8 sts)
Rnds 1 and 2 *P5, k1, p1, k1; rep from * to end of rnd.
Rnd 3 *K5tog, k1, M1P, (p1, k1, p1) in next st, M1P, k1; rep from * to end of rnd.
Rnds 4–8 *P1, k1, p5, k1; rep from * to end of rnd.
Rnd 9 *M1P, (p1, k1, p1) in next st, M1P, k1, k5tog, k1; rep from * to end of rnd.
Rnds 10–12 Rep Rnd 1.
Rep Rnds 1–12 for Pod Stitch.

COWL
Cast on 80 sts. Place marker for beg of rnd. Join by working the first st on left hand needle with the working yarn from the right hand needle and being careful not to twist sts.
Work Rnds 1–12 of Pod Stitch twice (24 rnds total), then work Rnds 1–10 once more.
Bind off.

FINISHING
Weave in ends.•

Garfield Ridge Afghan

● Basic

MEASUREMENTS
Approx 45 x 60"/114.5 x 152.5cm

MATERIALS
Yarn
LION BRAND® Homespun® Thick & Quick®, 8oz/227g skeins, each approx 160yd/146m (acrylic/polyester)
- 3 skeins in #437 Dove (A)
- 6 skeins in #211 Granite Stripes (B)

Needle
- One size 50 (25mm) circular needle, 40"/101.5cm long, *or size to obtain gauge*

Notion
- Tapestry needle

GAUGE
3½ sts = approx 4"/10cm over St st with 3 strands held tog using size 50 (25mm) needle. *BE SURE TO CHECK YOUR GAUGE.*

NOTES
1) Afghan is worked in one piece with 1 strand of A and 2 strands of B (3 strands total) held together in Stockinette st (k on RS, p on WS) with Garter st (k every st on every row) borders.
2) As you knit, be sure to always work the sts through all 3 strands.
3) Afghan is worked on a circular needle to accommodate the large size sts. Work back and forth in rows on the circular needle, just as if working on straight needles.
4) For our sample Afghan, we made sure that both strands of B began at the same point in the color sequence.

AFGHAN
With 1 strand of A and 2 strands of B held together, cast on 40 sts.

Lower Border
Knit 8 rows for Garter st border.

Row 1 (WS) K4 (for Garter st side border), p to last 4 sts (for St st center of Afghan), k4 for side border.
Row 2 Knit.
Rep Rows 1 and 2 until piece measures approx 54"/137cm from beginning, end with a Row 1 as the last row you work.

Top Border
Knit 8 rows.
Bind off.

FINISHING
Weave in ends.●

Mitford Hood

Basic

MEASUREMENTS
Circumference Approx 21"/53.5cm
Height Approx 17"/43cm

MATERIALS
Yarn
LION BRAND® Wool-Ease® Thick & Quick® Bonus Bundle®, 12oz/340g skeins, each approx 212yd/194m (acrylic/wool)
• 1 skein in #154 Grey Marble

Needles
• One pair size 13 (9mm) knitting needles, *or size to obtain gauge*

Notion
• Tapestry needle

GAUGE
9 sts = approx 4"/10cm in Garter st using size 13 (9mm) needles.
BE SURE TO CHECK YOUR GAUGE.

NOTE
Hood is worked as a rectangle, then folded and seamed following diagrams below.

HOOD
Cast on 48 sts.
Work in Garter st (k every st on every row) until piece measures approx 17"/43cm from beginning.
Bind off.

FINISHING
Following diagrams, fold and seam piece.
Weave in ends.•

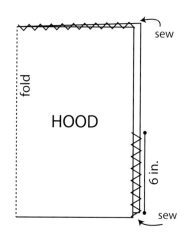

Classic Ribbed Hat & Scarf

Basic

MEASUREMENTS
Hat
Circumference Approx 19"/48.5cm, will stretch to fit a range of sizes
Height Approx 11½"/29cm
Scarf
Approx 8 x 58"/20.5 x 147.5cm

MATERIALS
Yarn
LION BRAND® Wool-Ease® Thick & Quick® Bonus Bundle®, 12oz/340g skeins, each approx 212yd/194m (acrylic/wool)
• 1 skein each in #617 City Lights (A) and #109 Petrol Blue (B)

Needles
• One pair size 13 (9mm) knitting needles, *or size to obtain gauge*

Notion
• Tapestry needle

GAUGE
9 sts = approx 4"/10cm over Rib pat using size 13 (9mm) needles.
BE SURE TO CHECK YOUR GAUGE.

NOTES
1) Hat and Scarf are each worked in one piece with 2 colors of yarn.
2) Hat is worked flat and then seamed.
3) When changing yarn color on Scarf, carry unused color of yarn along side edge of work until next needed.

HAT
With A, cast on 44 sts.
Work in Rib pattern as follows:
Row 1 (WS) P4, *k3, p3; rep from * to last 4 sts, k4.
Row 2 K the knit sts and p the purl sts.
Rows 3–5 With A, rep Row 2.
Change to B.
With B, rep Row 2 until piece measures approx 9"/23cm from beginning, end with a WS row (a row that begins with p4) as the last row you work.

Shape Crown
Dec Row 1 (RS) K4, *p2tog, p1, k3; rep from * to last 4 sts, p2tog, p2—you will have 37 sts.
Rows 2, 4, and 6 K the knit sts and p the purl sts.
Dec Row 3 K4, *p2tog, k3; rep from * to last 3 sts, p2tog, p1—30 sts.
Dec Row 5 K1, *k2tog, k1, p1; rep from * to last st, p1—23 sts.
Dec Row 7 K1, *k2tog, p1; rep from * to last st, p1—16 sts.
Cut yarn, leaving a long yarn tail.
Thread tail through remaining sts, pull to close top of Hat and knot.

Thread yarn tail into tapestry needle and sew sides of piece together. Weave in ends.

SCARF
With A, cast on 33 sts.
Work in Rib pattern as follows:
Row 1 (WS) P3, *k3, p3; rep from * to end of row.
Row 2 K the knit sts and p the purl sts.
Rows 3–5 With A, rep Row 2.
Join B and begin stripe pattern.
Stripe Rows 1 and 2 With B, rep Row 2.
Stripe Rows 3 and 4 With A, rep Row 2.
Rep Stripe Rows 1–4 until Scarf measures approx 56"/142cm from beginning, end with Rows 1 and 2 (a B stripe) as the last 2 rows you work. Cut B.
Last 5 Rows With A, k the knit sts and p the purl sts.
Bind off.
Weave in ends.•

Reading Room Cardigan

Easy

SIZES
S/M (L/1X, 2X/3X).

MEASUREMENTS
Bust Approx 40 (48, 56)"/101.5 (122, 142)cm
Length Approx 29 (30, 31)"/73.5 (76, 78.5)cm

MATERIALS
Yarn
LION BRAND® Wool-Ease® Thick & Quick® 6oz/170g skeins, each approx 106yd/97m (acrylic/wool) (6)
• 8 (10, 12) skeins in #154 Grey Marble

Needles
• One size 13 (9mm) circular needle, 29"/73.5cm long, *or size to obtain gauges*

Notions
• Stitch markers
• Stitch holders
• Tapestry needle
• 5 buttons, approx 1¼"/32mm diameter
• Sewing needle and thread

GAUGES
8 sts + 18 rows = approx 4"/10cm in garter st using size 13 (9mm) needle.
8 sts + 14 rows = approx 4"/10cm in St st using size 13 (9mm) needle.
BE SURE TO CHECK YOUR GAUGES.

NOTES
1) Cardigan is worked sideways in one piece, beg at one sleeve edge. The sleeve is worked, then sts are cast on for the back and the left front. Work continues in one piece until the left front and back are divided to shape the neck.
2) Sts are cast on for the right front and this piece is worked separately, then joined to the back. The join is made by simply working across the sts of the right front, then continuing across the sts of the back (no sewing is involved in this join!). Work then continues in one piece across the back/right front and the second sleeve.
3) A circular needle is used to accommodate the width of the fabric. Work back and forth in rows on circular needle as if working with straight needles.
4) Cardigan is worked in garter st (k every st on every row) and St st (k on RS, p on WS).
5) The gauge difference between St st and Garter st gives a slight A-line shape to the Cardigan.

KNIT CAST-ON
*Insert right needle in next st on left needle; wrap yarn and pull through (as if knitting a st); transfer new st to left needle; rep from * for desired number of sts.

CARDIGAN
Cast on 22 (24, 26) sts.
Purl 1 row.

Left Sleeve
Beg with a RS (knit) row, work in St st for 16 rows.
Increase Row (RS) K1, kfb, k to last 2 sts, kfb, k1—24 (26, 28) sts.
Work in St st for 9 (7, 5) rows.
Rep Increase Row—26 (28, 30) sts.
Rep last 10 (8, 6) rows until you have 28 (32, 36) sts.
Work in St st for 6 rows.
Ridge Row (WS) Knit.
Work in St st for 2 rows.
Rep Increase Row—30 (34, 38) sts.
Ridge Row (WS) Knit.
Work in St st for 3 rows.
Ridge Row (WS) Knit.
Rep last 4 rows once more.
Work in St st for 2 rows.
Rep Increase Row—32 (36, 40) sts.
Next Row (WS) Knit.

Cast-on for Back and Front
Using Knit Cast-On, cast on 42 sts for back—74 (78, 82) sts.
Row 1 (RS) Knit.
Using Knit Cast-on, cast on 42 sts for left front—116 (120, 124) sts.
Row 2 P34 (36, 38) for St st lower front of Cardigan, k24 for garter st upper front of Cardigan, place marker for center of shoulder, k24 for garter st upper back, p34 (36, 38) for St st lower back.
As you continue to work, slip the marker on each row as you come to it.
Row 3 Knit.
Row 4 P34 (36, 38), k48, p34 (36, 38).

Reading Room Cardigan

Rep Rows 3 and 4 until the garter st upper front section measures approx 7 (8½, 10)"/18 (21.5, 25.5)cm from cast-on sts, end with a WS row as the last row you work.

Divide at Neck for Left Front and Back
Row 1 (RS) Work sts as established (in St st and garter st) to marker, then slip these 58 (60, 62) sts to a holder for back, bind off 2 sts, work sts as established to end of row—you will have 56 (58, 60) sts rem on needle, these sts are the left front.

Left Front
You will now be working over left front sts only.
Next Row (WS) Work sts as established (in St st and garter st) across.
Decrease Row K2tog, work sts as established to end of row—55 (57, 59) sts.
Rep last 2 rows 2 more times—53 (55, 57) sts.
Work in established sts until upper left front garter st section measures about 9¼ (11¼, 13¼)"/23.5 (28.5, 33.5)cm from cast-on edge.

Button band
Work in Garter st for 7 rows.
Bind off.

Back
Slip sts for back from holder onto needle and join yarn so that you are ready to work a WS row.
Decrease Row (WS) K2tog, work sts as established to end of row—57 (59, 61) sts.
Work sts as established for 26 (30, 34) rows.
Increase Row (RS) Work in established patterns to last 2 sts, kfb, k1—58 (60, 62) sts.
Slip sts to a holder.

Right Front
Cast on 53 (55, 57) sts.

Buttonhole Band
Knit 3 rows.
Buttonhole Row (WS) K8, *k2tog, using Knit Cast-on, cast on 1 st, k6; rep from * 3 times, k2tog, using Knit Cast-on, cast on 1 st, k to end of row.
Knit 3 rows.

Next Row (WS) P34 (36, 38) for St st lower front, k to end of row for garter st upper front.
Work sts as established for 4 (6, 8) rows.
Increase Row (RS) K1, kfb, work in established patterns to end of row—54 (56, 58) sts.
Next Row Work sts as established.
Rep last 2 rows 2 more times—56 (58, 60) sts.
Next Row (RS) Using Knit Cast-On, cast on 2 sts, work in established patterns to end of row—58 (60, 62) sts.

Join Right Front and Back
Next Row (WS) Work sts as established across right front, k24 back sts from holder, p rem 34 (36, 38) back sts from holder—116 (120, 124) sts.
Work sts as established until right front measures same as left front, end with a WS row as the last row you work.

Right Sleeve
Next 2 Rows Bind off 42 sts, k to end of row—32 (36, 40) sts rem.
Decrease Row (RS) K1, k2tog, k to last 3 sts, k2tog, k1—30 (34, 38) sts.
Work in St st for 2 rows.
Ridge Row (WS) Knit.
Work in St st for 3 rows.
Rep Ridge Row.
Rep last 4 rows once more.
Rep Decrease Row—28 (32, 36) sts.

Work in St st for 2 rows.
Rep Ridge Row.
Work in St st for 6 rows.
Rep Decrease Row—26 (30, 34) sts.
Work in St st for 9 (7, 5) rows.
Rep Decrease Row—24 (28, 32) sts.
Rep last 10 (8, 6) rows 1 (2, 3) more times—22 (24, 26) sts rem.
Work in St st until right sleeve measures same as left sleeve.
Bind off.

FINISHING

Sew side seams. With sewing needle and thread, sew buttons to left front button band opposite buttonholes.

Neck Edging

From RS, pick up and k36 (40, 44) sts spaced as evenly as possible around neck edge. Without working any rows, bind off all sts as if to knit. Weave in ends.•

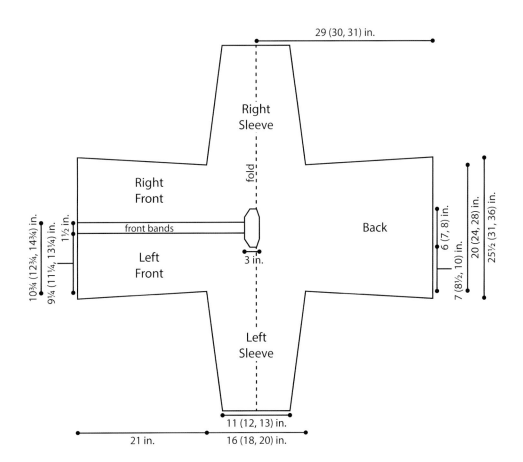

Hudson Cowl

Easy

MEASUREMENTS
Circumference Approx 34"/86.5cm
Height Approx 8"/20.5cm

MATERIALS
Yarn
LION BRAND® Wool-Ease® Thick & Quick®, 6oz/170g skeins, each approx 106yd/97m (acrylic/wool)
• 2 skeins in #610 Hudson Bay

Needle
• One size 13 (9mm) circular knitting needle, 29"/73.5cm long, *or size to obtain gauge*

Notions
• Stitch marker
• Tapestry needle

GAUGE
8½ sts = approx 4"/10cm over Rnds 1–4 of cowl pattern using size 13 (9mm) needle. *BE SURE TO CHECK YOUR GAUGE.*

NOTE
Cowl is worked in one piece in the round on a circular needle.

COWL
Cast on 72 sts.
Place marker for beginning of rnd and join by knitting the first st on the left hand needle with the working yarn from the right hand needle and being careful not to twist the sts.
Rnds 1 and 2 Knit.
Rnds 3 and 4 Purl.
Rnds 5–36 Rep Rnds 1–4.
Rnds 37 and 38 Rep Rnds 1 and 2.
Bind off.

FINISHING
Weave in ends.•

3 Strand Grande Shawl

Easy

MEASUREMENTS
Approx 23 x 75"/58.5 x 190.5cm

MATERIALS
Yarn
LION BRAND® Homespun® Thick & Quick®, 8oz/227g skeins, each approx 160yd/146m (acrylic/polyester)
• 4 skeins in #213 Antique Stripes (A)
LION BRAND® Homespun®, 6oz/170g skeins, each approx 185yd/169m (acrylic/polyester)
• 2 skeins in #309 Deco (B)

Needle
• One size 50 (25mm) circular needle, 24"/61cm long,
or size to obtain gauge

Notion
• Tapestry needle

GAUGE
4 sts = approx 4"/10cm over St st with 3 strands held tog using size 50 (25mm) needle. *BE SURE TO CHECK YOUR GAUGE.*

NOTES
1) Shawl is worked in one piece with 2 strands of A and 1 strand of B (3 strands total) held together in St st (k on RS, p on WS) with Garter st (k every st on every row) borders.
2) A circular needle is used to accommodate the large stitches. Work back and forth on circular needle as if working on straight needles.
3) As you knit, be sure to always work the sts through all 3 strands.

SHAWL
With 2 strands of A and 1 strand of B held together, cast on 24 sts.

Beginning Border
Knit 6 rows for Garter st border.

Row 1 (WS) K3 (for Garter st side border), p to last 3 sts (for St st center of Afghan), k3 (for Garter st side border).
Row 2 Knit.
Repeat Rows 1 and 2 until piece measures approx 71"/180.5cm from beginning, end with a Row 1 as the last row you work.

Ending Border
Knit 6 rows.
Bind off.

FINISHING
Weave in ends.•

High Plains Scarf

Easy

MEASUREMENTS
Approx 7 x 55"/18 x 140cm

MATERIALS
Yarn
LION BRAND® Wool-Ease® Thick & Quick® Bonus Bundle®, 12oz/340g skeins, each approx 212yd/194m (acrylic/wool/rayon)
• 1 skein in #123 Oatmeal

Needles
• One pair size 35 (19mm) knitting needles, or size to obtain gauge

Notion
• Tapestry needle

GAUGE
6½ sts + 8 rows = approx 4"/10cm over pat Rows 1–4 with 2 strands of yarn held tog using size 35 (19mm) needles.
BE SURE TO CHECK YOUR GAUGE.

NOTE
The Scarf is worked in one piece with 2 strands of yarn held together. To work with 2 strands, you can use the yarn strand from the outside of the yarn ball and the yarn strand from the center of the ball, or you can simply wind the yarn into 2 equal size balls before beginning.

SCARF
With 2 strands of yarn held together, cast on 11 sts.
Rows 1 and 2 Knit.
Row 3 P1, *k1, p1; rep from * across.
Row 4 K1, *p1, k1; rep from * across.
Rep Rows 1–4 until about 1yd/1m of both strands of yarn remains, ending with a Row 2 as the last row you work. Bind off.

FINISHING
Weave in ends.•

Quick Seed Stitch Cowl

Easy

MEASUREMENTS
Circumference Approx 27"/68.5cm
Height Approx 10½"/26.5cm

MATERIALS
Yarn
LION BRAND® Wool-Ease® Thick & Quick®, 6oz/170g skeins, each approx 106yd/97m (acrylic/wool)
- 1 skein in #138 Cranberry

Needle
- One size 13 (9mm) circular needle, 16"/40.5cm long, or size to obtain gauge

Notions
- Stitch marker
- Tapestry needle

GAUGE
8 sts + 15 rnds = 4"/10cm over Rnds 1 and 2 using size 13 (9mm) needle.
BE SURE TO CHECK YOUR GAUGE.

NOTES
1) Cowl is worked in the round on a circular knitting needle.
2) Edges of Cowl will roll gently to create an interesting edge.

COWL
Loosely cast on 53 sts. Place marker for beg of rnd and join by working first st on left-hand needle with working yarn from right-hand needle and being careful not to twist sts.
Knit 5 rnds.
Rnd 1 K1, *p1, k1; rep from * around.
Rnd 2 P1, *k1, p1; rep from * around.
Rep Rnds 1 and 2 for 12 more times.
Knit 5 rnds.
Bind off loosely.

FINISHING
Weave in ends.•

Snowball Hat

Easy

MEASUREMENTS
Circumference Approx 17½"/44.5cm, will stretch to fit a range of sizes
Length Approx 8"/20.5cm

MATERIALS
Yarn
LION BRAND® Wool-Ease® Thick & Quick®, 6oz/170g skeins, each approx 106yd/97m (acrylic/wool) (6)
• 1 skein in #099 Fisherman

Needles
• One set (5) double-pointed needles (dpn) size 15 (10mm),
or size to obtain gauge

Notions
• Stitch marker
• Pompom maker
• Tapestry needle

GAUGE
10 sts = approx 4"/10cm over pat Rnd 1 using size 15 (10mm) needles.
BE SURE TO CHECK YOUR GAUGE.

NOTES
1) Hat is worked in one piece in the round on double pointed needles.
2) Pompom is tied to the top of the finished Hat.

HAT
Loosely cast on 44 sts. Divide sts evenly over 4 needles with 11 sts on each needle.
Place marker for beginning of rnd and join by working the first st on the left hand needle with the working yarn from the right hand needle and being careful not to twist sts.
Rnd 1 *K1, p1; rep from * around.
Rep Rnd 1 until piece measures approx 7"/18cm from beginning.

Shape Crown
Next Rnd K2tog around—you'll have 22 sts.
Next Rnd K2tog around—you'll have 11 sts.
Next Rnd Knit the first st, then k2tog around—you'll have 6 sts.
Cut yarn, leaving a long yarn tail. Thread yarn tail into blunt needle, then draw through remaining 6 sts and pull to close the top of Hat. Knot securely.

FINISHING
Following package directions, make a large pompom and tie to top of Hat.
Weave in ends.•

Betania Cardigan

●●● Intermediate

SIZES
X/S (M/L, 1X/2X).

MEASUREMENTS
Bust 40 (49, 58)"/101.5 (124.5, 147.5)cm
Length 32 (34, 36)"/81.5 (86.5, 91.5)cm

MATERIALS
Yarn
LION BRAND® Wool-Ease® Thick & Quick®, 6oz/170g skeins, each approx 106yd/97m (acrylic/wool)
- 5 (6, 7) skeins in #149 Charcoal (A)
- 4 (5, 6) skeins in #612 Coney Island (B)
- 2 (3, 3) skeins in #609 Moonlight (C)
- 3 (3, 4) skeins in #535 River Run (D)
- 1 (2, 2) skeins in #154 Grey Marble (E)

Needles
- One size 11 (8mm) circular knitting needle, 40"/101.5cm long, *or size to obtain gauge*
- One size 13 (9mm) circular knitting needle, 32"/81.5cm long

Notions
- Stitch markers
- Stitch holders
- Tapestry needle

GAUGE
9 sts + 12 rows = approx 4"/10cm in St st using larger needles.
BE SURE TO CHECK YOUR GAUGE.

STITCH GLOSSARY
M1 (make 1) An increase worked by lifting the horizontal strand lying between needles and placing it onto the left needle. Knit this new stitch through the back loop—1 st increased.

K1, P1 RIB
(worked over an odd number of sts)
Row 1 K1, *p1, k1; rep from * to end of row.
Row 2 K the knit sts and p the purl sts.
Rep Row 2 for K1, P1 Rib.

NOTES
1) Cardigan is worked in 5 pieces: Back, Left Front, Right Front, and 2 Sleeves.
2) Yarn colors are changed to make stripes.
3) Stitches for the front bands and collar are picked up along front edge Cardigan.
4) Front bands and collar are shaped by working short rows. Short rows are rows that are worked over a portion of the sts in a row, leaving the remaining sts unworked. To work short rows, the pattern instructions will tell you to "turn" before you reach the end of the row.
5) A circular needle is used to accommodate the number of sts. Work back and forth with the circular needle as if working on straight needles.
6) When you see "as established" in the instructions, this means to continue in the current pattern st. For example, to continue in a rib pattern, k the knit sts and p the purl sts.

STRIPE SEQUENCE
*Work 12 rows with A, 14 rows with B, 8 rows with C, 10 rows with D, 6 rows with E; rep from * for Stripe Sequence.

CARDIGAN
Back
With smaller needle and A, cast on 55 (65, 75) sts.

Lower ribbing
Row 1 (RS) With A, work Row 1 of K1, P1 Rib.
Rows 2–12 Continue in K1, P1 Rib changing color following Stripe Sequence.

Body
Change to larger needle.
Changing color following Stripe Sequence, work in St st (k on RS, p on WS) until piece measures approx 4"/10cm above rib, end with a WS row as the last row you work.
***Dec Row (RS)** K1, k2tog, k to last 3 sts, ssk, k1—53 (63, 73) sts.
Continue in St st, changing color following Stripe Sequence, for 4"/10cm, end with a WS row as the last row you work.
Rep from * 3 more times—47 (57, 67) sts.
Rep Dec Row—45 (55, 65) sts.
Continue in St st, changing color following Stripe Sequence, until piece measures approx 32 (34, 36)"/81.5 (86.5, 91.5)cm from beg.
Bind off.

Betania Cardigan

Pocket Linings (make 2)
With larger needle and D, cast on 17 sts.
Work in St st until piece measures approx 9 (10, 11)"/23 (25.5, 28)cm from beg, end with a WS row as the last row you work. Place these sts on a holder.

Left Front
With smaller needle and A, cast on 25 (29, 33) sts.

Lower ribbing
Row 1 (RS) With A, work Row 1 of K1, P1 Rib.
Rows 2–12 Continue in K1, P1 Rib changing color following Stripe Sequence.

Body
Change to larger needle.
Continue to change color following Stripe Sequence.
Row 1 (RS) K5 (7, 9), pm, work in K1, P1 Rib as established over next 17 sts, pm, k3 (5, 7).
Row 2 P to marker, sm, work in K1, P1 Rib to next marker, sm, p to end of row.
Row 3 K to marker, sm, work in K1, P1 Rib to next marker, sm, k to end of row.
Row 4 P to marker, sm, work in K1, P1 Rib to next marker, sm, p to end of row.
Rows 5–14 Rep last 2 rows 5 more times.
Dec Row 15 K1, k2tog, k to marker, sm, work in K1, P1 Rib to next marker, sm, k to end of row—24 (28, 32) sts.
Rows 16–29 Rep Rows 2–15—23 (27, 31) sts at the end of Row 29.
Rows 30–31 (30–33, 30–35) Rep Rows 2 and 3 for 1 (2, 3) times.

Join pocket lining
Remove markers while working next row.
Row 32 (34, 36) P to marker, bind off 17 sts between markers, p to end of row.
Row 33 (35, 37) K to bound-off sts; from RS, k across sts of one Pocket Lining from holder, k to end of row.
Next 9 (7, 5) rows Work in St st.
Dec row 43 K1, k2tog, k to end of row—22 (26, 30) sts.
Rows 44–48 (44–54, 44–56) Work in St st for 5 (11, 13) rows.

Size XS/S ONLY—Shape neck
Row 49 K to last 3 sts, ssk, k1—21 sts.
Work in St st for 7 rows.
Row 57 Rep Row 43—20 sts.
Row 58 Purl.
Row 59 Rep Row 49—19 sts.
Work in St st for 9 rows.
Row 69 Rep Row 49—18 sts.
Row 70 Purl.
Row 71 Rep Row 43—17 sts.

Size M/L ONLY—Shape neck
Row 55 K to last 3 sts, ssk, k1—25 sts.
Row 56 Purl.
Row 57 Rep Row 43—24 sts.
Work in St st for 7 rows.
Row 65 Rep Row 55—23 sts.
Work in St st for 5 rows.
Row 71 Rep Row 43—22 sts.

Size 1X/2X ONLY—Shape neck
Row 57 Rep Row 43—29 sts.
Work in St st for 3 rows.
Row 61 (RS) K to last 3 sts, ssk, k1—28 sts.
Work in St st for 9 rows.
Row 71 K1, k2tog, k to last 3 sts, ssk, k1—26 sts.

All sizes
Work in St st for 7 (3, 9) rows.
Row 79 (75, 81) K to last 3 sts, ssk, k1—16 (21, 25) sts.
Work in St st for 9 rows.
Row 89 (85, 91) K to last 3 sts, ssk, k1—15 (20, 24) sts.
Note For the next line of instructions, "0" repeats means that for your specific size you should not perform that particular instruction, just skip to the next part of the instructions.
Rep last 10 rows 0 (1, 1) more time(s)—15 (19, 23) sts.
Work even in St st until piece measures same as Back. Bind off.

Right Front
Cast on and work in rib as for Left Front.

Body
Change to larger needle.
Continue to change color following Stripe Sequence.
Row 1 (RS) K3 (5, 7), pm, work in K1, P1 Rib as established over next 17 sts, pm, k5 (7, 9).
Row 2 P to marker, sm, work in K1, P1 Rib to next marker, sm, p to end of row.
Row 3 K to marker, sm, work in K1, P1 Rib to next marker, sm, k to end of row.
Row 4 P to marker, sm, work in K1, P1 Rib to next marker, sm, p to end of row.
Rows 5–14 Rep last 2 rows 5 more times.
Dec Row 15 K to marker, sm, work in K1, p1 Rib to next marker, sm, k to last 3 sts, ssk, k1—24 (28, 32) sts.
Rows 16–29 Rep Rows 2–15—23 (27, 31) sts at the end of Row 29.
Rows 30–31 (30–33, 30–35) Rep Rows 2 and 3 for 1 (2, 3) times.

Join Pocket Lining
Remove markers while working next row.
Row 32 (34, 36) P to marker, bind off 17 sts between markers, p to end of row.
Row 33 (35, 37) K to bound-off sts; from RS, k across sts of 2nd Pocket Lining from holder, k to end of row.
Rows 34–42 (36–42, 38–42) Work in St st for 9 (7, 5) rows.
Dec Row 43 K to last 3 sts, ssk, k1—22 (26, 30) sts.
Rows 44–48 (44–54, 44–56) Work in St st for 5 (11, 13) rows.

Size XS/S ONLY—Shape Neck
Row 49 K1, k2tog, k to end of row—21 sts.
Work in St st for 7 rows.
Row 57 Rep Row 43—20 sts.
Row 58 Purl.
Row 59 Rep Row 49—19 sts.
Work in St st for 9 rows.
Row 69 Rep Row 49—18 sts.
Row 70 Purl.
Row 71 Rep Row 43—17 sts.

Size M/L ONLY—Shape Neck
Row 55 K1, k2tog, k to end of row—25 sts.
Row 56 Purl.
Row 57 Rep Row 43—24 sts.
Work in St st for 7 rows.
Row 65 Rep Row 55—23 sts.
Work in St st for 5 rows.
Row 71 Rep Row 43—22 sts.

Size 1X/2X ONLY—Shape Neck
Row 57 Rep Row 43—29 sts.
Work in St st for 3 rows.
Row 61 (RS) K1, k2tog, k to end of row—28 sts.
Work in St st for 9 rows.
Row 71 K1, k2tog, k to last 3 sts, ssk, k1—26 sts.

All sizes
Work in St st for 7 (3, 9) rows.
Row 79 (75, 81) K1, k2tog, k to end of row—16 (21, 25) sts.
Work in St st for 9 rows.
Row 89 (85, 91) K1, k2tog, k to end of row—15 (20, 24) sts.
Rep last 10 rows 0 (1, 1) more time(s)—15 (19, 23) sts.
Work even in St st until piece measures same as Back.
Bind off.

SLEEVES (make 2)
With smaller needle and A, cast on 25 (27, 29) sts.
Work in rib as for Back.
Change to larger needle.
Continuing to change color following Stripe Sequence, work in St st for 3 rows.
Inc Row K1, M1, k to last st, M1, k1—27 (29, 31) sts.
Rep last 4 rows 11 (12, 13) more times—49 (53, 57) sts.
Work even in St st until piece measures about 23"/58.5cm from beg.
Bind off.

FINISHING
Sew shoulder seams.

Front Bands and Collar
Note Do not wrap stitches before turning work for a short row—this design works beautifully without the wraps.
Row 1 (RS) From RS with smaller needle and A, beg at lower right front corner, pick up and k 1 st in end of each row along right front edge to beg of neck shaping, pm, pick up and k 1 st in end of each row to right shoulder, pick up and k 1 st in each st across back neck, pick up and k 1 st in end of each row from left shoulder to beg of neck shaping, pm, pick up and k 1 st in end of each row along left front edge to lower left front corner. Pick up an additional st if needed to ensure that you have an odd number of sts.
Work back and forth in rows on circular needle as if working with straight needles. Slip markers as you come to them.
Row 2 Work Row 1 of K1, p1 Rib.
Row 3 Work in K1, P1 Rib.
Row 4 Work in K1, P1 Rib to 10 sts before 2nd marker (marker on right front), TURN.
Row 5 Work in K1, P1 Rib to 10 sts before next marker (on left front), TURN.
Row 6 Work in K1, P1 Rib to end of row.
Row 7 Work in K1, P1 Rib.
Row 8 Work in K1, P1 Rib to 8 sts before 2nd marker (marker on right front), TURN.
Row 9 Work in K1, P1 Rib to 8 sts before next marker (on left front), TURN.

Betania Cardigan

Row 10 Work in K1, P1 Rib to end of row.
Row 11 Work in K1, P1 Rib.
Row 12 Work in K1, P1 Rib to 6 sts before 2nd marker (marker on right front), TURN.
Row 13 Work in K1, P1 Rib to 6 sts before next marker (on left front), TURN.
Row 14 Work in K1, P1 Rib to end of row.
Row 15 Work in K1, P1 Rib.
Row 16 Work in K1, P1 Rib to 4 sts before 2nd marker (marker on right front), TURN.
Row 17 Work in K1, P1 Rib to 4 sts before next marker (on left front), TURN.
Row 18 Work in K1, P1 Rib to end of row.
Row 19 Work in K1, P1 Rib.
Row 20 Work in K1, P1 Rib to 2 sts before 2nd marker (marker on right front), TURN.
Row 21 Work in K1, P1 Rib to 2 sts before next marker (on left front), TURN.
Row 22 Work in K1, P1 Rib to end of row.
Row 23 Work in K1, P1 Rib.
Row 24 Work in K1, P1 Rib to 2nd marker (marker on right front), TURN.
Row 25 Work in K1, P1 Rib to next marker (on left front), TURN.
Row 26 Work in K1, P1 Rib to end of row.
Bind off in rib.

Sew in Sleeves. Sew Sleeve and side seams.
Sew Pocket Linings to WS of Fronts.
Weave in ends.•

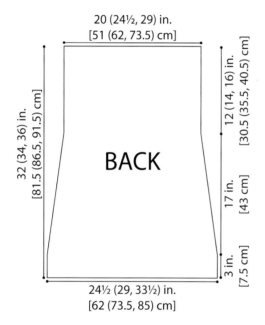

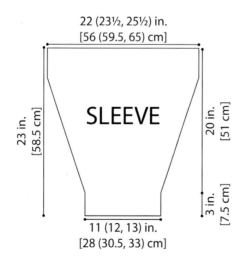

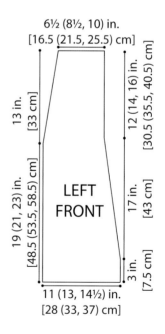